D1744113

Davenport's NORWICH

Davenport's
NORWICH

by George Nobbs and Hamilton Wood
WENSUM BOOKS

WENSUM BOOKS (NORWICH) LTD
33 ORFORD PLACE, NORWICH NOR 06D

© 1973 WENSUM BOOKS (NORWICH) LTD

ISBN 0 903619 08 3   (Paperback)

Acknowledgements

We would like to express our gratitude to those people who have helped us in the preparation of this book. A full list of 'credits' appears elsewhere, but we would especially like to thank Mrs Heather Davenport, not only for allowing us to reproduce a great deal of her late husband's work in her possession, but also for her constant help, advice, and encouragement.

Norwich School of Art, where Dav spent so many years of his working life, also gave us assistance and encouragement – Bill English, David Jolley and Alan Everington deserve special mention.

Many people answered an appeal for paintings and although we were unable to use all the pictures offered, we are most grateful to all the people who took the trouble to get in touch with us.

Eastern Counties Newspapers made photographs available to both us and Norwich School of Art and we gratefully acknowledge their permission to reproduce the picture which appears on pages 2 and 3. We discovered the story of Mr Barry and the Porch of St Andrew's Hall in 'Norwich Inheritance' and are indebted to the authors of that book for recording it.

We would like to thank Mr Philip Hepworth, the City Librarian, and the staff of Norwich Central Library for answering our many queries. Our publishers, too, deserve special thanks for their support and enthusiasm for this book. Those individuals who have worked behind the scenes, often at short notice, in order to assist in this book's publication are listed in the 'credits' and we are most grateful to them as we are to the staff of our printers.

Finally we would like to thank all our other friends who have given advice and help.

GEORGE NOBBS
HAMILTON WOOD

5

List of Credits

Text pages 26 to 78: George Nobbs

Text pages 10 to 22: Hamilton Wood

Photography: Rodney Tompson

Copy Preparation: Ken Cooper

Cover Design: Colin Baldwin

Jacket notes: Tom Wright

Edited and Designed by George Nobbs

Produced by Wensum Books

Photograph on pages 2 and 3 courtesy of Eastern Counties Newspapers Ltd

Pictures on pages 42 and 74 courtesy of Mr and Mrs R. J. Mitchell

Picture on pages 40 and 41 courtesy of Mr J. F. C. Mills

Picture on pages 72 and 73 courtesy of Mrs Howard Brown

All other pictures reproduced by courtesy of Mrs Heather Davenport

Introduction

It is ironic that this book, like the retrospective – now titled 'Memorial' – exhibition of Dav's work, should appear some eight months after his death. It means little to say that the exhibition was planned a year ago and that Dav had made a list of pictures to be included in it; or to say that I had talked often to Hamilton Wood about this book and that just before Christmas we had decided to discuss it with Dav when we next all met up in a pub. His illness at the beginning of this year persuaded us to postpone approaching him on the subject until he recovered. Sadly he never did.

It was only a couple of days after Dav's death that I spoke to Hamilton Wood and the book came up in conversation again. Clearly now, I thought, the book would never be published – Hamilton Wood disagreed and thought that it could serve as a tribute to him. It was then largely due to the encouragement of Heather Davenport that we decided to revive the idea and with her help we were able to make the selection of her late husband's work which appears in this book. Our only regret is that Dav did not know that this work would appear.

But such a book as this could not have worked if it had not been for the fact that Dav, Hamilton Wood, and I all seem to see Norwich in the same way. For us the City does not consist only of Elm Hill, the Cathedral and such-like. It is also a place of factories, bomb-sites, car parks and back alleys. That is what Dav painted and what I wanted to write about. It is curious that I have recently found an article written by John Piper in late 1943 and published in the *Cornhill Magazine* of January 1944. It is on the subject of Norwich and Piper discusses the view from Whitefriars Bridge, where Jarrolds' factory stands.

To Piper the view was 'more Norwich-like and more exciting then the overdone plaster houses of Elm Hill, or any other picturesque bits. The view looking westwards along the besmirched river, shows steam exhausts from brick-built factories blowing out above the water by timber yards and derelict sites. On the banks and beyond rise the flint towers of churches, and the irregular blocks of factories and warehouses. . . .

'It is views like this, not quaint views of old-world cobbled streets, that really make Norwich residents abroad feel a nostalgia for home. They may not explain it for themselves, but it is so. It is the kind of view that is forgotten at committee meetings of even the best-intentioned preservation societies.'

It is strange that an outsider could so quickly grasp, and so eloquently express, what we feel about the City depicted in 'Davenport's Norwich'.

Finally I must point out that Mr Wood has written an account of Dav's life and that I am responsible for the text which accompanies the pictures. The opinions expressed in that text is mine alone and does not necessarily reflect the views of my fellow-writer and friend Hamilton Wood.   GEORGE NOBBS

7

Davenport, Man and Artist

by Hamilton Wood

Buried deeply, but still active in the collective unconscious of Norwich is the memory of itself as the third (or was it the second?) city of the kingdom. Buried even more deeply is the destruction of the Saxon city's identity by the Normans and the displacement of the centre to the neighbourhood of their castle. Its most abiding characteristics are its local pride and independence, which seem to combine with the very architecture and geography of the place to yield the special flavour of living there; this is an easily acquired taste. Norwich itself has a strong, often posthumous, regard for citizens of high achievement, like John Crome the painter, for example. Likewise it looks with affection upon its 'characters' – Billy Blue Light, a popular eccentric of the last century, is still affectionately recalled by older inhabitants.

Leslie Davenport wasn't a native of Norwich but he virtually became one. He arrived from London via Oxford in 1943. He worked and played equally hard during the subsequent thirty years of change. He left a large body of work recording much of this change from a city predominantly of bricks and flint to one of considerable concrete. Life's plums and honours largely passed him by but he gave and received much loyalty and affection. He was both artist and character and it's difficult to say which came first.

He lived just long enough to learn that the school of art to which he had given so much devotion was about to honour him with a large retrospective exhibition during the Norwich Triennial Festival of 1973. 'I always said that if you work hard you get there in the end, man' was his characteristic comment on this. In the event it was to be a posthumous exhibition. His funeral congregation filled both the north and south transepts of Norwich Cathedral. Had there been time to let everyone know (and had the funeral not coincided with the City versus Spurs League Cup Final at Wembley – he was a City supporter himself) it might have filled the nave as well.

The Twenty Group

I first met him in 1948. There was a 'working evening' of the Norwich Twenty Group in the old Garth buildings at Norwich School of Art and some of us were laying out for mutual appraisal the things we had been doing when this genial bald-headed character dropped in. He didn't say very much – he never did, really – but glanced and smiled at the faces and the work, returning almost at once to his life class, whence he had slipped away during the model's interval. 'Who's that?' I asked (I was new to the scene, having only just returned to Norwich). 'Oh,' they said, 'That's Mr Davenport.'

This Norwich Twenty Group was the brain-child of one Walter Watling, who conceived it as something similar to the group of artists surrounding John Crome of Norwich a century or so before. They were to be closely associated in their work and would collaborate by discussion for mutual improvement. It was to be limited to twenty members (hence the name) to simplify communication and to maintain standards. In his musings Watling recalled that Crome's society met in pubs, as the Twenty Group was to do, but he forgot to cast somebody in the role of John Crome.

Simple Yet Complex

The group survived surprisingly well for a brain-child, and through many vicissitudes, but often its success had to be ascribed to Davenport, who became its staunchest member. 'The Twenty Group was Dav', they were saying shortly after his death. But Dav wasn't just the Twenty Group; there was more to him than that, more facets to his marked single-mindedness. 'He was the most complicated simple man I ever knew,' said Heather, his widow.

She was able to say this because she had seen him in most of his roles, in each of which, taken alone, he cut the simple uncomplicated figure. Davenport the teacher, for example, was a feature of Norwich Art School for a quarter of a century. Faithful, kindly, hard-working, he exuded a simple, steady enthusiasm which especially endeared him to students. Although essentially well informed, he stood out as honest and unsophisticated during the turmoil of a bewildering succession of movements and changes in the world of the artist, all proclaiming authenticity. Davenport of artists' societies like the Norfolk and Norwich Art Circle was a similar figure, who, here among a predominantly amateur membership, carried the authority of the professional but with no trace of snobbery. There were other Davenports too; the father-figure of a ramifying family, for example, or the man of strenuous and often uproarious leisure.

The Works of Man and Nature

But simplicity and single-mindedness were most marked as features of his art and of his methods. Simplicity for him didn't mean simplification by abstraction, as it might have done for an artist of his time. It meant seeing and accepting what was there, often enough steel scaffolding or gasometers, building contractors' litter, such things as he was wont to call 'the works of man, man' (one always got addressed as 'man', whether one was a man or a woman). This simplicity became forthrightness, and then, having committed himself to a forthright statement in a sketch, he set forth with even more forthrightness upon a painting, sometimes arriving at what seemed to be an overstatement but never at a jaded version of the first idea.

Davenport rarely explained a point of view. He very clearly had a philosophy but he was by no means philosophical. The 'works of man' was a category

11

which remained undefined and included not only the creative works (largely in ferroconcrete) but also the destructive works of man. When he arrived in Norwich the city had suffered, in common with Bath, Dresden, and many of man's beautiful urban achievements, the ingenious and ferocious consequences of man at war. He accepted the bomb-sites and the drabness almost without comment and set to work to transmute them into art. He built no articulated aesthetic philosophy out of this situation; he simply used it to make pictures. Later, when reconstruction became a public preoccupation, he became the rather more articulate advocate of 'modern' (ferroconcrete) buildings for the city.

Looking at this city today it may be difficult to visualize it in the late forties, when the twentieth century had scarcely as yet left any creative mark except the Swedish-orientated City Hall of the late thirties. The war and the reconstruction had helped the community to become aware of its rich medieval and Georgian inheritance and the notion of town-planning was becoming a popular concern. But there were few who looked beyond the prospect of conservation and the architectural concept of 'keeping in keeping', and fewer still bold or brash enough to advocate or even to predict the arrival on the scene of concrete tower blocks. When Davenport did so it sounded either funny or outrageous.

Above the city on the north-east side rise the gravel hills of Mousehold Heath. It is famous as a place from which to view the townscape. An eighteenth-century print called *A South-west Prospect of the City of Norwich* is still very popular and even today the main features of the ancient walled city may still be recognized. In the nineteenth century John Crome painted the view from these breezy uplands. In the twentieth the city erected there a memorial to the writer R. H. Mottram who promoted the now-plagiarized phrase 'A fine city, Norwich.' Towards the end of his career Davenport was commissioned to make a painting of the scene from the same place as John Crome. The site was the same, the task was different, for the tower blocks which he had once so wildly advocated now adorned the view.

This task was doubly poignant for Davenport. He loved Mousehold, and often painted there, but not the works of man. He had, although he never enbalmed it in a phrase, a great love of the works of nature too. It was a vigorous unsentimental love; nature was a tonic and a respite. 'A brisk walk over Mousehold, man' was his prescription for all the ills that flesh is heir to, and those of the spirit also. He even used it for an overdose of alcohol at a party, and fell down a pit, emerging scratched and bruised and, characteristically, highly amused.

The Outdoor Davenport: Foibles and Fun

The outdoor Davenport was a strange mixture of foibles and fun. An example of the former was his principle of always shaving outdoors in every weather and season. It was a ritual acknowledgement of the pre-eminence of the elements. Man should strive to try himself against them. Real men lived in the Stone Age; men of the Age of Concrete should aspire to similar hardihood. There was an unwritten, unspoken mythology to all this; somewhere way back in the remote past, so he once hinted, he had belonged to an outfit called the Kibbu Kift. It

12

seems to have been a sort of youth and woodcraft movement of his early years, and it left its mark, hence Davenport the camper. He started it; many years ago he set forth with his children and a bell tent, patriarchally, to establish a new way of life among the mud-flats, streams, and dunes of the North Norfolk coast. Others followed; an *ad hoc* tribe sprang up. The tribe was transhumant; they wintered in the city, mostly as artists, in summer they trekked to the wilderness. They moved to the heaths and woodlands of Sizewell on the Suffolk coast. A concrete nuclear-power station sprang up and drove Davenport of the Kibbu Kift north again. Finally they descended to the Great Valley at Winterton-on-Sea and this became their summer territory for fifteen years.

You didn't go camping, you went to camp, like you go to church (here endeth the resemblance). It was an informal society with tribal elements. The region was wild in those days, and Davenport used to renegotiate the territory every year with Edward Bush, chief of a pre-cast concrete manufactory just inland. Children ran wild and one only heard about their adventures years later. In fine weather they slept out under the stars in a great huddle on the high dunes with Davenport's dog in the middle. Institutions sprang up: plays and entertainments were improvised in a natural amphitheatre in the dunes. Everyone contributed to a 'camp magazine' which ranged from the sublime to the scurrilous. A tatterdemalion sports day always happened, among other, unplanned happenings. It was all rough and tough and friendly, with music, feuds, and fun. Come hell or high water Davenport kept to his regimen. In the mornings he set forth to paint, clad and equipped in a manner between Van Gogh and Cézanne. At three o'clock in the afternoon, whatever the state of tide and weather, he set forth to swim, sometimes with a trail of followers, always with Fred, his dog. I have seen him set off across the dunes on his own, running with legs like sticks of celery (he never sun-bathed) through a hail- and thunderstorm.

In the evening everyone repaired to the pub. Winterton had a long history of fishing and seafaring, of beach-sloop rescues and near piracy, of smuggling and general daredevilry, and it had all left its mark in the Fisherman's Return. Davenport, with his weather-beaten face, his white beard, and the fringe of hair round his brown baldness above his hairy jersey, was often taken for an old salt himself. Sometimes he played along, and earned pints from summer visitors for telling unlikely yarns.

Lord of Misrule

This was Davenport the figure of fun, Lord of Misrule. He always got away with it; this was his style. In later years he smoked a decorated clay pipe. Innocents would ask the old salt what he smoked in it, especially if they were pipe-smokers themselves. 'Rabbit droppings,' he would reply, 'gather them every morning on the dunes, man.' Then, aided by the atmosphere and the alcohol, he ardently advocated the adoption of this health-promoting habit and, finally, when he judged that his arguments and his own apparent folk-wisdom and longevity had sufficiently eroded the incredulity of his applicant he would pull out a pouch of the things and ply him with them. He claimed occasional successes.

13

His fun was methodical, like his art. There was some principle involved called 'working it all out', but this did not imply planning the fun beforehand; it meant inducing a catharsis, getting rid of repressions and frustrations, usually through singing. For a long time he put in constant and faithful attendance at the performances of a banjo band called the Muttonchops, whose sound had the right cathartic properties. At other times Davenport himself provided the sound; it was one of his little rituals. He was a specialist, and his repertoire seemed not to extend beyond three songs, which remained forever new, like fairy-stories. The best known was a concoction called 'I'm the Sheik of Araby', of which the refrain ran 'I've got no pants on' (in order to make the thing scan, the accent had to fall upon the 'on' and this became part of the musical clowning). It was loud, it was monstrously ridiculous, and it was infallible: it always stole the show, and the one who always enjoyed it most was Davenport.

His painting was methodical, sustained, and deliberate. The last thing you could imagine him doing with paint was mindlessly throwing it around, much as he might advocate vigour of handling and richness of impasto. But he never verbally condemned any movement in painting (or any painter for that matter). He did regard Impressionism as played out, and himself as essentially modern.

Visits to London

At intervals he took flying visits to London to catch up with the scene. These were breathless occasions and, if you accompanied him, great tests of physical as well as aesthetic endurance. He saw the lot, and on the hoof. You fed on snacks from your pocket as you raced along. If you were lucky you paused for a beer. If you were not and it was hot and there were more than the usual number of galleries to be inspected, you felt as if you had dragged your tongue along the pavement the whole way. But Dav was happy. 'First class, man,' he would remark at the end of the adventure.

People remarked from time to time that this pursuit of contemporary ideas seemed to have no visible effect upon his own art. It is true that he made more effort than most to keep up to date, but he was typically a man of effort, making more effort than most about everything, after his own fashion. It would have been quite unlike him to have adopted someone else's theories about his art and to have changed his style and his ways accordingly. For that matter, he attended practically every one of the Twenty Group's art forums for nearly thirty years, and in this way he heard more comments upon his work from other people than most artists do, yet his work never showed any revolutionary changes.

The First Norwich Period

Some change there was, nevertheless. In general it was a movement towards stronger and stronger assertion, greater conviction in what he saw and painted. Three broad 'periods' may be discerned in his work since his arrival in Norwich. In the 1940s he was making watercolours. By comparison with his later work they are surprisingly gentle. The first I ever saw, though not till years later, was a

14

sketch of that secluded flinty corner of Bishopsgate where the Adam and Eve public house stands, a glimpse of the world of Anthony Trollope. Yet soon his colleagues of the time were becoming slightly alarmed by what they considered to be 'distortions' appearing in his work, by a new boldness which disturbed the sequestered Norwich art scene.

He became disturbingly omnivorous in his subject-matter. He began to record the beauty of gasometers and vacant lots as often as that of accredited antiquities. By the 1950s he had entered his 'middle period'. In a mixed exhibition Davenport had become something of a menace; the size, the hardness, the clarity of light and shadow were shouting down his co-exhibitors. It all culminated in a great exhibition of concrete at the Assembly House in 1967. Chunks of it seemed to jut out from the walls of the gallery. You felt in danger of barking your shins if you moved unwarily.

The Unofficial War Artist

Undoubtedly this corresponded with the pace of architectural change in the city. The motor car was proving more relentless than the Nazi bombers. The place was being gutted for it. Roadworks, multi-storey parks appeared while high-rise flats and bulky new edifices like Prospect House, the Stationery Office building and its precincts challenged the Cathedral. The skyline from Mousehold recorded the change like a barometric profile of the weather. Down in the sweet Valley of the Yare at Earlham a jagged monument to the pace of change erupted as though to herald a new geological era. And Davenport seemed to love it all. It was as if the rumblings of his early 'distortions' had been an omen. Where there was rubble and shuttering, there was Dav. Eyeshade and jerkin, easel and board, he embarked on his bike for the scene (he was a sworn enemy of the motor car). He became a well-known figure, as inevitable on a building site as the clerk of the works. He was the unofficial war artist of the battle of the old and the new.

The Third Period: 'Dear Old Dav'

Then gently and genially he slipped into his 'third period'. This more or less corresponded with his retirement from Norwich School of Art but its inception was no more definite than that event itself (he still returned to take part-time portrait classes, and even when these finished he continued to do the same work in premises provided for him at the Crome Centre). This was the period of 'dear old Dav'. His family seemed to extend to embrace a whole cluster of friends. He had moved to a house within the Cathedral lands in Bishopgate itself and within sight of the Cathedral, but also of the gasworks, one of his early loves and near by was Bishops Bridge, one of his very earliest.

He continued to paint, if anything more prolifically, but what he painted was more often the Cathedral and its precincts. The spire appeared in many pictures, but was generally glimpsed beyond something else, and, in several, clothed in scaffolding, recorded with typical Davenport relish. The back of his own house,

15

and the garden, which overlooked the Grammar School playing-fields, furnished him with material. There he grew sunflowers, and the sunflowers became almost a symbol of the period. They appeared as the chief feature of some pictures, with the buildings as background.

At the height of the rubble and concrete period, vegetation was more or less fugitive. It had never been a primary subject for him, except for a series of studies of a bush at this camping site which overlooked the sea and had grown crouched and bent in its defiance of the winds. These sunflowers were symbols of defiant vitality. They were larger than life. They were glorious and voracious vegetables celebrating life with sturdiness and confidence; and he painted them with all the confidence in his own draughtsmanship that his studies of buildings had bequeathed him. They were living architecture.

His last completed oil-painting was highly significant in relation to the main body of his work. It was of Pull's Ferry and the medieval watergate, one of the city's scenic celebrities, and one so frequently tackled by amateurs that professional painters tended to regard it as a hackneyed picturesque subject. Davenport took the medieval stone mass sideways, as if an experienced wrestler should startle an opponent with a new throw. A veteran, he had returned to the place where he started, to a Norwich antiquity, which, apart from preservation, the twentieth century had passed by. He took it by surprise, he stripped it of prettiness and he endowed it with strength, his strength and its own.

One of the Davenport archives is the diary in which he kept notes of the subjects he intended to tackle in the future. His work was always programmed in this way and in many other ways he was a man of method. We do not have to guess what he would have been doing next, and he always seemed confident in his intention to do it; there was always more life to come. If anyone ever mentioned death, his classic reply was, 'I'll see you under the sod, man.'

The Last Winter

The winter of 1972/73 was mild. A good winter for shaving out of doors. It should have been the winter of Davenport's content, for he had learned of the forthcoming retrospective exhibition at the Norwich School of Art, which meant recognition in an area which had too often ignored him for its other preoccupations. But those who knew him well began to notice something; the exuberance was withering; if asked to sing one of his raucous ballads at a party he declined, or performed only with an effort. He confronted this thing in the only way his philosophy sanctioned – he scorned medicine, like the motor car – he cycled up to Mousehold and drew deep breaths of the wind on that heath.

The last time I saw him he was in bed. His aged dog and cat were both with him. There was a wintry defiance in the eyes. One knew, whether one had seen this thing before or not, what it meant. He did not die of this affliction but of another which supervened. When he was moved to hospital he was in a coma, mercifully, for this, to him, would have been a final humiliation.

Two works formed an epilogue. One was a self-portrait. He did not paint portraits, although he taught many the art, and a self-portrait was above all

16

uncharacteristic. This was drawn from the bedroom mirror and was faint to the point of ghostliness, but was a fully evocative image, an impression unlike anything else he ever did, a poignant image of the end. The other is an unfinished landscape sketch. He had rallied slightly before the last, had called for his drawing-board, and gone to the window (open of course) and remarked 'Must keep your hand in, man.'

His Place and Time in Art

He left behind a large volume of work, the product of a relentless routine. Davenport never waited for inspiration; he was no painter of moods. Yet he was in some way an 'original', rather in the French sense. His style was unmistakable, but difficult to analyse because technically there is little difference between his work and methods and those of the average conventional landscape-painter. It is rather that he did it so much and so persistently that a style emerged from the work, as a craftsman's workmanship develops a style over the years.

Could he have a place in the history of art people have sometimes asked. Perhaps a minor niche, possibly more, but the question is wrongly put. It should really be – what is his time in the history of art? He belongs, most emphatically (*le mot juste*, in Davenport's case) to the world of Post-Impressionism. He was born in 1905, the year before Cézanne died and two years before Picasso painted the epoch-breaking *Les Demollisees d'Avignon*. He died a few weeks before Picasso. Cézanne had succeeded in his aim of making 'something enduring' of Impressionism, of putting structure and material back into its tremulously atmospheric world. With *Les Demoiselles* Picasso splintered the tradition. The final development of this tradition had been Impressionism. It was here that Davenport came in. He was quite sure that Impressionism was dead even if it wouldn't lie down.

One upshot of these events was Cubism, the chunky geometrical reconstruction of the world which led straight towards abstract art. This, in Davenport's formative years, when in England C. R. Nevinson was painting works like *La Mitrailleuse* to celebrate the mechanical fury of the First World War, would have been the progressive movement. At one time in Norwich Davenport was paying rather thin lip-service to abstraction, as if it were a moral obligation which carried no real conviction for him. (Once, in the mid 1950s, he actually tried to 'go abstract', using motifs from Norwich Fairground – it didn't work for him.) If only he had remarked that his real aim was 'to put reality back into Cubism' this would at once have provided a convenient historical hook on which to hang his pictures, and an explanation of his style. But he did not; indeed among all his gruff aphorisms none referred directly to his own art.

He lived through a strange time, when art itself seemed to be in a perpetual state of self-doubt, ceaselessly seeking new forms. After the invention of Cubism, Picasso spent the rest of his career doing just this, seeking new forms. Much of the activity seemed to be clowning. Indeed there was a very powerful clown inside Picasso, and one inside Davenport also, the other side of whose nature in some ways resembled that of Cézanne.

Norwich, Europe, War and Peace

If all this was so, why did he come to Norwich, and not settle in London or Paris? Whatever the material reason, Norwich was a strangely appropriate choice. It had itself nourished its own artistic tradition. Norwich is one of those cities, like Florence or Haarlem, which has done this. Nobody would suggest that Davenport had encountered the Norwich School, had felt in sympathy with its naturalism, had supposed that some of its tradition still survived and realized that the city itself was about to encounter the turmoil of twentieth-century rebuilding, which would supply him with appropriate material, and settled there accordingly, but he settled there just the same. That's the way the cookie crumbled. He settled in Norwich and made occasional forays on London, and once, at least, in a spirit of high jinks, on Paris.

He adopted provincial Norwich, but Norwich did not adopt him all at once. Indeed at times Norwich treated him rather as Aix treated Cézanne. It absorbed him slowly, the more digestible parts first. When he arrived, there was a war on, but Norwich had seen the worst of it through. It had suffered its bit in the great game of techno-military tit for tat, Bath, Coventry, and Churchill's 'roofless Lübeck'. The bonfires of Dresden were yet to be, and Norwich was keeping its head down in the centre of a great land-based aircraft-carrier. (Davenport had spent some time in an aircraft factory at Bristol and some of the sketches he made of aircraft in construction are still extant.)

But soon the dust had settled and two documents emerged. One was Kent and Stephenson's *Norwich Inheritance*, a record of, and a plea for, the historic beauties of the place to which urgent attention had to be drawn. The other was the 1945 *Norwich Plan* which, if it did nothing else, sowed the seed of the idea of change. The battle of the bulldozers was soon to be engaged.

The Cultural Inheritance

There was another Norwich inheritance too, which did not get recorded in a new definitive book. This was a cultural inheritance, a consciousness that Norwich had, in the late eighteenth and early nineteenth centuries been called 'the Athens of the North', nurturing intellectuals and people of social and cultural consciousness – John and Amelia Opie, Harriet Martineau, William Taylor and his circle, Dr Rigby and Frank Sayers, the Fry and Gurney families. It had produced writers and artists like George Borrow, John Crome, and John Sell Cotman. In the twentieth century the internationally famous Maddermarket Theatre of Nugent Monck had been established here (Davenport was as staunch a supporter of the Maddermarket as at one time time of the football team; every performance he saw there was 'first class, man').

By Davenport's arrival the knowledge of this inheritance was largely in the guardianship of what Mr Eric Fowler once called 'the two hundred', a culturally conscious élite. Davenport was a rough diamond for this setting, and a maverick intellectual like Reyner Banham got a bit of a raw deal. Professor Bernard Meadows, Norwich born, once offered to write on 'the meanness and insularity of Norwich regarding the visual arts'. This was long before the erection of his

18

monumental phallus at Prospect House confounded this and any other assertion that Norwich looked backwards.

Art, Architecture, and the Future

Indeed shortly after the war it began to awaken from the privations to share the near-universal feeling that there could be a future, not only without grim frugality in material things but with room for cultural expansion. Rather incoherently at first, an awareness of the possibility of a new style of living began to emerge. Life might even be leavened with a little frivolity once more. Seriously, there could be fun. What was Picasso doing now, apart from designing doves of peace? One looked around.

The prevalent views in the visual arts are a good indicator of the life-style of a period. This is especially so in notions of design. The processes of reappraisal in the 1930s had eventually crystallized into the Puritan doctrines of Functionalism. It was sinful to decorate. Victorian and Edwardian exuberance had been the Sodom and Gomorrah of designers. Functionalism was a convenient ideology with which to survive a war. Virtue lay in plainness and rationality. It had emerged triumphantly afterwards in the Utility ranges of goods. But functional utility was only an expedient. Presently the fun party began to emerge.

Suddenly the Government itself attempted a great leap forward. A State-sponsored pleasure-dome and other delights were decreed on the South Bank of the Thames. It was 1951; the second half of the twentieth century was upon us, its future fears and sorrows and frustrations concealed by a mood of restive enthusiasm which saw the brighter side of its possibilities.

Davenport could not wait. He saw the inside of that Dome long before it was finished. In London on one of his gallery-viewing expeditions he led his small party down through the builders' mud and rubble, under the barricades to have a look at the future. We carried sheaves of papers under our arms to evade suspicion through the semblance of office.

The general atmosphere was one of released optimism. The world of the artist began to stir; the movements got moving again and proliferated. Monolithic figures like Henry Moore were challenged by young men with quite different materials and different ideas. It became increasingly apparent that the artistic melting-pot was moving from Paris to London and New York.

Town, Gown, and Twenty Group

Back in Norwich there were stirrings too. It was a do-it-yourself movement here. There was public tolerance but little official support or, as yet, municipal initiative. A typical enterprise of the period was the organization of outdoor shows of painting and sculpture in the Castle Gardens. They were more like a market in their bustle and informality. It was our own idea, our own enterprise, and our own work. When later the City bought one of those municipal status symbols, a Barbara Hepworth sculpture, it was erected here as if to mark the spot.

There was in fact something sadly symbolic in this act. The local enthusiasts had broken the ground, had shown the way, had demonstrated that enthusiasm aroused more enthusiasm, and that the public could be aroused from apathy and scepticism to a genuine interest in the arts. The municipal response, however, was to turn away from this local enterprise and towards the central artistic establishment. Davenport, among others, was dismayed, and was to have cause for further dismay, but his stubborn high spirits always carried him through.

Wherever there was enterprise, there was Davenport, in some place like the Cathedral cloister hanging paintings for the Twenty Group, or at the Norwich School of Art, putting them up for the Arts Council. This art school, which occupied more than simply his working life, was typical of many up and down the country. Most towns had one, and didn't clearly know why. Actually they were mainly established in response to the great furore about standards of industrial design in the nineteenth century. These standards could somehow be maintained and improved by fostering awareness through knowledge, not only of the 'applied', but of the 'fine' arts.

In the 1950s Norwich School of Art was being benevolently and tolerantly administered by Mr Noel Spencer, a Principal who was much concerned with the human side of such institutions. As a result it was regarded with a good deal of affection by its students and there was a ready town-and-gown *rapport*. This was particularly felt at the open meetings of the Twenty Group, where in addition to the inevitable Davenport himself, there were bound to be one or two members of the art school staff. These meetings, in pubs like the Sir Garnet Wolsey and the Festival House, ranged in atmosphere from the intellectual intensity of a university seminar to the bibulous conviviality of a bar-room discussion, and could sometimes be conducted with critical ferocity. Davenport loved them, and indeed they did become very popular, partly as a serious forum and partly as entertainment. There's great sport in watching to see whether someone's picture is going to be praised or pilloried.

Occasionally there were bizarre episodes. One evening for instance at the Sir Garnet Wolesley Mr Nightingale turned up. Mr Nightingale had run an art shop in Elm Hill since well before the war, when Elm Hill was nothing like as genteel as it is now. There was a Left Bank atmosphere about him and there is no doubt that he had authentic knowledge of the living art of his period. He was said to have known personally George Bernard Shaw and other celebrities of his time. He was also a close friend of certain people like the pet-shop keeper who made the atmosphere of Elm Hill noisome with the effluvia of the offals upon which he fed the pets, but who endeared himself to Mr Nightingale through that great social catalyst, drink.

On this occasion he hadn't got the pet-shop keeper in tow, but an antique-dealer whom he was calling 'the Major'. When they appeared at the top of the short flight of stairs somebody called 'Ah, Mr Nightingale, do come and help us discuss this picture.' He wended his way forward, although there was room enough and he had no need to wend; he peered at the picture and said, 'Well, I don't know what you think, Major' (the major didn't tell us either), 'but I think it's – I think it's' (there came the sound of arrested unvoiced labio-dental fricatives), 'shorry, ladish preshent, no, can't poshibly . . .'. Finding himself thus verbally inhibited he fell back upon gesture and moved his hands around the surface of the unfortunate painting with such panache and aplomb that it was difficult to tell whether the silence which fell when he had finished was a tribute to his exposition or regret that it had ever started.

There were many such enlivening and enlightening incidents at these meetings down through the years. Davenport seemed to prefer the enlivenment – 'Practically a punch-up last night, man, damn good meeting.' Not that he ever made any acerbic criticisms himself, for he was generally encouraging to everybody in a gruff sort of way. The meetings flourished and became a social institution, but things were changing elsewhere.

Metropolitan Sophistication and the Provincial Wilderness

The fearful fifties passed into the swinging singing sixties. It all went to the head in London, where everything that was anything was deemed to happen. Fringe rabble from the central scene sometimes penetrated the provincial wilderness as far as Norwich where, if not immediately honoured for their metropolitan pre-eminence, they attempted to poison the water-holes of the natives. The Twenty Group was one such oasis.

Changes, too, were happening in the art school world. The mild benevolent régime of Noel Spencer came to a close just at the time of the first rumbles. Something called the Summerson Committee had decreed that art schools must vie for something called 'Recognition'. The fruits of recognition were to be honour, glory, and expansion; those of non-recognition were assignment to the wilderness. The mountains were in labour.

This process in Norwich was presided over by an able administrator hot-foot from London, John Brinkley. The process of king-making which succeeds a new head appointment in such institutions was short and effective. Recognition was in the air, was within reach, and was attained. As far as the art-citizens of Norwich were concerned it meant that the primary local connection was reduced in favour of joining the national network. When the position was consolidated John Brinkley achieved a *rapprochement* with the local scene. He had consented to open the Annual Exhibition of the Norfolk and Norwich Art Circle at the Castle Museum in 1968 when suddenly and sadly he died.

The Twenty Group was licking its wounds. A bunch of Red Guards, arrogantly confident that it was an anachronism, had made the monthly forum untenable for a time, having fortified their courage at the expense of their wits with liberal libations in the bar before their assaults began. But exhibitions continued and meetings recovered during a quiet aftermath when John Fox presided over the destinies of the Norwich School of Art and Davenport over those of its part-time classes, which remained as a local connection. He retired but continued to serve these classes as a part-time tutor himself. Finally, in the summer of Mr Fox's departure, in 1972 these classes were closed. Coincident with the appointment of the new principal came the announcement of the retrospective Davenport exhibition in the school, which seemed like a recognition not only of the artist himself but, by implication, of the existence of the local art scene.

Art, Life, Style, and the Man

By virtue of his industry, his fortitude, his independence, and his individuality Davenport became for a time a symbol of that scene. He forged a style and a method which extended from his work to his life and to himself. By being so much himself he gathered others round him. He didn't have imitators and he didn't found a school. The scene and the time didn't throw up a new John Crome but it did produce a figure who was always so much there, being himself, that when he departed some people felt as if the Rock of Gibraltar had suddenly been removed.

Art may sometimes seem susceptible to analysis; life is not, and is often best related in anecdotes. It was characteristic of Davenport that he went his own way, be believed his own thing, he did his own singing, he framed his own pictures, arranged his own exhibitions. He made no high-falutin principle of it, but he was always ready to perform services for colleagues. He was, for example, a reliable source for artists' models. He brought his own style to this service and always kept his north eye on potential material. He would recruit 'characters' for portrait classes from the street, from the pub, from where he saw them. Nudes were more dicey. Having opened the subject, he would pop the question: 'Costume or life, man?' ('life' being a euphemism for the nude).

He lived at one time in Victoria Street, through which some immigrant Italian workers who lived in the neighbourhood passed on their way to work or to church. When they were in good heart they would sing in the street, great swelling Neapolitan songs. Several beautiful girls, returning from church, passed his house one Sunday lunchtime. Davenport was about to carve the chicken. 'Just look at those girls, Dav,' someone said. 'My God, first-class models, man,' he cried, leaping for the door, carving-knife still in hand. He was always more honest than subtle in his approach ('guileless', as Noel Spencer put it). 'Hi!' he called, 'hi! hi!', as the girls fled, mute with terror at the sight of the knife, with Davenport still in pursuit.

It's there in the anecdote: the style, the man, the enthusiasm of the pursuit, not to mention the lovable element of the bizarre. No doubt this sort of episode may reinforce the Gully Jimson image of artists which some people, non-artists, of course, are sometimes tempted to form. But Gully Jimson is an archetypal caricature, and ever since Joyce Carey invented him his readers have been on the look-out for him in real life.

Artists, and people who know artists well, are aware that there is no such single type. They come in all sorts of clothes, have all sorts of manners and outlooks, but usually they are strongly individual, and are tolerant of individuality. This characteristic may have emerged from their working conditions in the latter-day Western tradition. Theirs is a one-man, one-job, one-style situation. They sometimes unite loosely in movements, but not in orchestras or teams or production lines. They have a way of living which they have won for themselves down the centuries, from Michelangelo's declaration 'I am not a shopkeeper' to Van Gogh's views on 'la vie d'artiste'. 'A picture,' it was once said, 'is a corner of life seen through a temperament.' Davenport's main *oeuvre* was a corner of life called Norwich in the mid twentieth century, seen through a temperament which was dogged, lusty, likeable, and independent.   H.W.

Davenport's Norwich

by George Nobbs

A selection of paintings of Norwich by the late Leslie Davenport together with a brief description of the scenes depicted.

overleaf: *St. Stephen's Church and Curls bomb site, painted in* 1947.

St Stephen's Church and Curls Bomb Site 1947 (overleaf)

Curls and Burlington Buildings early 1950s (opposite)

The war hit Norwich harder than most people had expected and now realize. In 1942, in a series of devastating raids, 2,000 houses were totally destroyed and 30,000 out of a total of 35,000 were damaged. The north and west of the City suffered worst with a third of our industrial capacity being lost, but in the heart of Norwich several shops were hit, such as Boots and Curls.

Fortunately the end of the war saw us still possessing our Castle, Cathedral, City Hall, Guildhall, Assembly House, most of our ancient streets and nearly all our three dozen pre-Reformation churches.

In the first years of peace a new building began to take shape.

Designated grandly 'Redevelopment Area Number One' by the Council, it was in fact Curls new shop rising from the rubble of the City's most spectacular bomb crater. A large hole situated on the site of a Victorian department store, it had become something of a local landmark ever since it was used as a static water tank and an enterprising American Serviceman had swum across it.

The 1945 Town Plan – a most significant document drawn up in 1944 as a blueprint of the post-war City – envisaged the area as a civic square with a fountain in the centre, but economic sense prevailed and this site, probably the most commercially valuable in the City, was built upon. It was also a good propaganda exercise to give the people back a large store in the centre of the City; it marked a return to normality and the building site in Orford Place became a popular attraction to the public who stood transfixed as they watched the progress of reconstruction.

Across the road in Rampant Horse Street, Buntings former shop was repaired and became the premises of Marks & Spencers, Woolworths moved into a new store next door and by the mid 1950s Orford Place was back to normal. And, most amazingly, the minor architectural gems that surrounded the site were still intact. The superb range of Edwardiana facing Curls had survived completely. It had been built as a complete street at the turn of the century and contained some of the best examples of its style to be found anywhere. Opposite, tucked away in a corner as a result of the new Curls, stood Burlington Buildings designed in 1904 by J. Owen Bond. In its new setting it reminds me of something that Dickens said of a house that had hidden in a corner when it was very small and had become trapped there as it had grown up.

The new Curls building hides one of the most interesting features of Burlington Building – its mock-balconies supported by figures of very bored-looking goddesses.

26

Davenport/55.

The Guildhall and Market-Place c. 1944/5

This is one of Dav's earliest-known pictures of Norwich. It was either painted during or just after the war because it shows the blast-walls which were erected round the ground floor of the Guildhall as they were round many public buildings. Only a few years previously, the whole area had been transformed by the redesigning of the Market-Place and the construction of the City Hall but Dav chose to illustrate this centuries-old aspect of Norwich instead.

The Guildhall itself was built between 1407 and 1453 to house the civic administration set up by the Charter of 1404. Its life has not been entirely uneventful; in 1511 the roof fell in, and in 1635 the hall itself started to totter when its foundations became undermined by enthusiastic saltpetre-diggers.

The nineteenth century saw some additions like the public clock which was put up in 1850 by Alderman Woodcock on condition that the Council remove the plaster ceiling inside and reveal the original timber roof. The Bassingham Gate was taken from a demolished building in London Street and incorporated into the west end of the south wall in 1857. In 1861 Thomas Barry, the City Surveyor, added the single-storey south wing to house the Victorian police station and in 1908 the Council were divided equally on a vote to pull the Guildhall down – the Mayor exercised a casting vote and the building was saved.

28

Barrack Street   1952

This picture of Barrack Street was painted in 1952 and shows part of the industrial side of Norwich. In the 1920s much of the street consisted of medieval houses which were quite rightly demolished in early slum-clearance schemes. The area of Pockthorpe, of which Barrack Street formed the centre, was one of the most socially underprivileged in Norwich and despite the efforts of people who lived there to make life a bit more cheerful – for example the Pockthorpe Guild complete with a Snapdragon – its demolition was long overdue.

The picture shows, on the left, the old Pockthorpe Brewery now occupied by Watneys, and in the foreground the Cavalry Barracks, built in 1791 and demolished in 1965.

Ketts Hill 1951

Dav's painting of Ketts Hill, taken from the same point as the picture of Barrack Street on the previous page but looking in the opposite direction and painted in the previous year, shows the Hill before the roundabout was built in 1954. In the foreground is the bakery and pub and to the left was once a small area of Victorian housing. Together this group made up 'Spitalfields', a development of 1823 which formed the first built-up area on this side of the river. It was over fifty years before there was any further building on Ketts Hill.

St Martin's At Palace Plain   c. 1947

Palace Plain, with its Church of St Martin is a typical corner of old Norwich. The church faces on its south side the gate to the Bishop's Palace and on its east side once stood the house of Sir Thomas Erpingham, who commanded the English archers at Agincourt and was immortalized by Shakespeare. When Dav painted this picture in the late 1940s the Gasworks stood where once Erpingham's house had been, but now that too has gone.

On the north side of the Plain is a fine range of buildings and in the biggest of these lived John Sell Cotman who, in 1824, opened the house as a 'School for Drawing and Painting in Watercolours. Terms one guinea and a half the quarter'.

31

Maddermarket Alley: St John's Church 1950

There is a great deal of history associated with this small alleyway and its adjoining buildings. The Palace of the Dukes of Norfolk stood in St Andrew's Street at the foot of the alley and it was here that the Elizabethan Duke plotted his foolhardy piece of treason in planning to marry Mary Queen of Scots and make her ruler, with him, of England. His second wife, and Duchess, who died in 1563 is buried here in the church. The Duke was beheaded on Tower Hill.

Maddermarket Alley: Theatre 1971

Also in the alleyway is the Maddermarket Theatre, an amateur institution founded by Nugent Monck many, many years ago. Today it flourishes in premises that have been in their time, a warehouse, a Catholic chapel, and a Salvation Army citadel before being converted, internally, to a replica of an Elizabethan theatre.

The Roman Catholic Church of Saint John the Baptist at St Giles's Gates early 1950s

On a sunny day in the early 1950s Dav painted this picture of St John's Church from the building site of the Grapes public house which was then going up.

The story of the church is an entertaining one if only for the attitude of the fifteenth Duke of Norfolk (the present Duke's father) who caused it to be built and bore all the costs. It was begun in 1884 and the architects were George Gilbert Scott and John Oldrid Scott. However the Duke paid little attention to the business of building lines and as the structure began to take shape it became obvious that the church was going to exceed the area intended for it and occupy a part of the road. Naturally, Norwich Corporation asked that the work be stopped and the Duke sent this somewhat bizarre letter to the Lord Mayor:

You have in Norwich your magnificent Cathedral, one of the noblest examples of the grand Norman architecture that exists in England or in the world. You have a display of beautiful Perpendicular churches absolutely unmatched for the almost prodigious generosity which has scattered them about your streets in ever bewildering multiplicity, but I think I am right in saying that you have hitherto had no example of the pure and noble Early English style. That I have now in part supplied, and I ask to be allowed to complete the work. Norwich has got half my church. If it does not want the other half, perhaps I had better build it in some place which will appreciate it more. To me, of course, this result will be a disappointment. I think that the two halves of a church look better when they are joined together, than when they are many miles apart, and therefore, though some other place may gain what Norwich loses, my building will suffer disastrously.

If my proposed building does incroach or rather abut upon the street at one point, it will surely be obnoxious as an unfinished and unsightly end, waiting for better days and a builder more fortunate than I am to complete the structure.

The Corporation gave in and the work continued although it was not until 1910 that the church was completed.

It was built on the site of the City Gaol which was moved to Mousehold, from which position St John's can be seen to good advantage – as it can from almost everywhere else, for while the Cathedral is built in the valley, the Duke chose the highest site in Norwich for his Church.

34

35

The West Front of St Andrew's Hall 1971

St Andrew's Hall, once the Church of the Dominican Friars, looms dramatically above the pubs and shops of St Georges Street. Much of its present appearance is the work of Thomas Barry the Victorian City Surveyor who had previously added the police station to the Guildhall. Two years later, in 1863, he set to work on totally 'restoring' St Andrew's Hall. The West Front, shown in this picture, is largely of his own invention but his most controversial action was that of rebuilding the South Porch.

When it was completed the *Norwich Mercury* said this about Mr Barry and his work:

'As to the needless, utterly useless Porch, perishing to the audience while in the Hall with the cutting draught, and more destructive when they come out – cold, comfortless, miserable in its nakedness, and bare walls, with its open external portal, its iron gates preventing shivering females from seeking the only refuge in these corners – its end will come.

Built upon false foundations, supported by equally false representations, an excrescence dishonouring by its design as by its erection their original founder, what can be said of this offspring of false taste and false statement, except that it is the true child of such parents, neither useful nor ornamental, deformed and misshapen, its life can be but one of suffering – its last moment will be the happiest, the blithest of its existence.

The inhabitants of the Emerald Isle are so imaginative, it is said, and so unstable, that to blunder and mistake is their nature. Would it not be a wonder then, if the Surveyor of the City was different from his countrymen.'

Mr Barry, however, was not without humour. The name of the Editor of the *Norwich Mercury* was Bacon and on the corbels of the criticized South Porch there appear four pigs. The four designs show: a pig blowing his own trumpet, a pig playing an organ to admiring demons, a pig spitting out reptiles while devils suck out his brains, and a pig swallowing the restored West Front surrounded by devils. It is thought that these pigs *could* be an allusion to Mr Bacon.

37

Norwich Cathedral

Norwich Cathedral was begun in 1096 by Herbert De Losinga. The surname means 'flatterer' or 'liar' and it was justly earned. He bought his ecclesiastical appointment and others for his family and then was advised by King William Rufus to go to Rome and seek a pardon for his many financial offences. One of the penances imposed by the Pope was the task of building a new Cathedral in Norwich.

The site chosen, on the low-lying meadows by the river, was influenced by Norman strategy. The fortified Close occupied part of the Saxon town centre, all of the citizens' grazing-lands, and dissected the Saxon road system. Together with the near-by Castle, it gave the Normans complete control of the city as well as destroying the existing central area – thus increasing the commercial importance of the Norman township of Mancroft.

Over the centuries, the building grew in size as did the monastic and various other aspects of the medieval church.

I have written in another book, *Norwich, a City of Centuries,* the turbulent story of the Cathedral's relationship with the City and will not rehash it here. Today relations are happier and the people of Norwich now generously contribute to the upkeep of the building – an attitude of forgiveness which the present Bishop appreciates but which would have baffled De Losinga.

The picture opposite shows the spire from the garden of a house at the Bishopsgate end of The Close. This is the fourth such structure. The first was burnt down by the citizens in 1272, the second was blown down in a gale in 1362, and the third was struck by lightning in 1463. This one dates from 1480.

On the following page is a picture that was just made for Dav – the Cathedral in scaffolding. It shows repairs to the North transept, a part of the Cathedral which the public never sees for it faces the Bishop's garden and serves as his private entrance to the church.

Sweetshop at the End of The Close c 1970

There is much dignity and beauty in The Close; so many architectural styles are displayed there that a painter or writer would wonder where to start first. I am glad that Dav took the bull by the horns – or rather, in this case, by the tail – and went just outside The Lower Close and looked back at the little Victorian sweetshop that stands on the 'wrong' side of the gate. The seventeenth-century house on the left is safely inside the gateway that leads into the walled enclave. In medieval times The Close was walled and much of it still is, if you think about it. In fact, this shop is actually in The Close, too, and the remains of the wall can be seen behind houses in Bishopsgate.

Foundry Bridge c 1970

Foundry Bridge is my favourite city bridge. The painting shows the bridge and its partner, Thorpe Station – the two being inseparably linked. It was the building of the first Thorpe Station in the early 1840s that caused the wooden Foundry Bridge of 1810 to be reconstructed in iron and when the station was rebuilt in the 1880s, so was the bridge.

The present Thorpe Station was designed by J. Wilson, the Chief Engineer of the Great Eastern Railway Company and it was built by Youngs & Son of Norwich at a cost of £60,000. It was opened to the public on 3 May 1886.

The date of the construction of the bridge is more difficult to place. It was included in the Norwich Improvements Act which received the Royal Assent on 16 July 1879 and was built nine years later. A City Council Report of 17 January 1888, after it had been completed, stated 'The original estimate for the work was £13,000'; the actual cost was £12,032 11*s*. 4*d*. The width is fifty feet – five feet more than originally intended and the Great Eastern Railway Company contributed £1,200 towards the cost of the undertaking.'

43

Norwich Power Station 1952

This picture, painted in 1952, is tremendously evocative of its period – midway between the Festival of Britain and the Coronation. It has the quality of a poster of the time and depicts the Norwich Electricity Generating Station at Thorpe – 'Power for Britain' you can almost see the poster type proclaiming. The station was opened in 1926 at a cost of £300,000 and enlarged in 1938. There are programmes of the two events in Norwich Central Library which are well worth looking at for their period flavour. The Norwich Electricity Company was formed by a group of local worthies in 1892 and began operation in the following year from premises in Duke Street. The plant, which was designed by Laurence & Scott, was purchased by the Corporation in 1902 and Alderman Edward Wild – a Director of the Company became Chairman of the City Electricity Committee.

The opening of the Power Station in 1926 was a gala affair with 'conveyances' leaving the Guildhall at 10.45 to take guests to Thorpe. After elaborate ceremonials, the 'conveyances' took the guests back to St Andrew's Hall for a Civic Luncheon.

At the time the picture was painted, Dav was in his most enthusiastic 'works of man' phase and Britain was living in an era of power cuts (caused by fuel shortages, not strikes). These two facts probably account for the lyrical quality of the painting.

Peafield Mill 1969

Dav must have been very keen to capture this building for it stands in a part of Norwich which he seldom visited with his easel. Lakenham Mill is properly called 'Peafield Mill' for it stood among fields of peas which gave their name to this whole area when it began to be developed in Late Regency and Early Victorian times. Nowadays the area is called 'New Lakenham' and the Mill, which was built in 1824, is now being converted into a flat by the Corporation who have advertised for 'an eccentric' to live in it. A very large number of replies were received – but then 50 per cent of Norwich people consider themselves to be eccentric and the others 50 per cent are considered odd.

Getting back to the Mill, it contained, when new, three pairs of four and a half foot millstones. It ceased producing flour in 1870 and went in for the manufacture of animal foodstuffs until it was damaged by a fire just before the First World War. Then for a time it was used to house German prisoners of war. It was in 1922 that Mr Woodrow started milling flour here again using one electric motor to drive the sails. He soon installed more motors and removed the sails. Production ceased when the company moved their operations to King Street in the 1960s.

Victoria Cottage   1955

This house clearly fascinated Dav as much as it does me. It stands on the corner of St Stephen's Road and Victoria Street and was built in the first half of the last century, but that is all that I know about it really. The staff of the Colman and Rye Department of Norwich Central Library, who are nothing if not helpful in this type of query, could only tell me that it was there in the 1860s and that Thomas Priest lived there from 1863 till at least 1883. His relations lived near by and none of the family have occupations listed after their names, which is quite exceptional in mid-Victorian directories and suggests that they had money.

The chief charm of the place is the ornate balcony which is still there although the greenhouse disappeared some few years ago.

47

Houses in Chapel Field Road   1945

Painted in the summer of 1945 – in the weeks following the end of the war in Europe – this picture shows the fine range of Regency houses that stood in Chapel Field Road. In the 1820s there was a sudden spate of building outside the city walls. At St Giles's Gates West Pottergate sprang up; by Bishops Bridge Spitalfields was begun; by Ber Street Gates and St Catherine's Plain new houses were built in Lakenham and here, by St Stephen's Gates, the New City appeared.

These houses here are probably the first to be built outside the wall and certainly the closest for they backed on to the wall itself, a section of which can be seen appearing between the two houses on the left of the painting.

Over the centuries these fine houses had shielded the wall from the 'march of progress' and when they were demolished recently to make way for the all-devouring Inner Ring Road, large sections of the medieval wall were revealed. One round tower contained a bedroom door, a window, and a small chimney. During the course of 'restoring' the wall the Corporation decided, with a total lack of imagination, to destroy all this evidence of domestic occupation.

Chapel in the Field   1972

It was the growth of the Early Victorian suburb called, somewhat romantically, the 'New City' that caused this fine old Chapel to be built by the Congregationalists. It was designed by Joseph James of London, constructed by Horace Sexton of St Swithin's, Norwich, cost £3500, took fifteen months to complete, was opened on 12 October 1858, and demolished by Norwich Corporation in 1972.

The painting shows the last moments of the Chapel, for the demolition was being carried on as Dav painted.

48

The Glass Tower c 1966

In 1960 the 'Glass Tower' was built – that is the name by which it has always been known. Although the Norwich Union had already begun building their huge office blocks, it was this structure which became known as the City's first sky-scraper. Shortly after its completion Purdy's, a local catering firm which came to prominence at the beginning of the 1960s, opened a twenty-four-hour restaurant on the ground floor. The venture was not a success for, sadly, a minority of louts caused fights there nearly every night. Eventually Purdy's were forced to resort to normal opening hours and its social importance declined. But the place, when it was reasonably peaceful, did seem to my generation to symbolize an era.

Two other buildings appear in the picture, one the small Church of All Saints seems almost lost in its present setting – once it was thatched and stood in the narrow street of Westlegate surrounded by medieval houses with the Swine Market by the churchyard. In the foreground is Ashworths/Stannards restaurant. I understand that some of this building once formed part of the parsonage.

U.E.A. 1967

Down in the Valley of the Yare, between the villages of Earlham and Eaton, there stands a group of strange, eerie monuments. They are similar in style to the Aztec temples of Mexico and are thought by some to be a survival of some long-lost civilization. Archaeologists have been able to place the date of their construction somewhere about the seventh decade of the twentieth century but their original purpose remains a mystery.

These temples – if this is what they were – are inhabited at certain times of the year by a tribe of people whose clothing and general appearance indicate that they are not indigenous to Norfolk. Their strange rites such as the ceremonial 'Sit-in', Union Jack burning, and their many other bizarre activities are thought to be a throwback to a previous civilization but it is unlikely that they ever possessed the skill, energy, or wealth to construct the vast temples and palaces in which they now live.

Davenport./72.

Norwich Central Library   1972

Norwich Central Library stands surrounded by building of considerable merit. The Assembly House, the Church of St Peter Mancroft, the Guildhall, and the City Hall are its immediate neighbours and it is unlikely that anything could have looked good faced with that sort of competition.

Perhaps the aptest comparison is with the City Hall – essentially a modern building but deplored by the modern school of architects for its flamboyance, its theatrical effects, and its general good looks. But the City Hall gets away with it. It is attractive because it has employed a few tricks of the trade like the balcony, the flight of steps, and the heraldic bronze lions.

The Library has been designed with a sort of modernistic integrity. There is no adornment about it. It is frankly, almost bravely modern, and rather ugly.

But once inside those prison-like gates, the picture changes. Here the modern design comes into its own and the place is light and attractive and houses a first-class library service – which really makes it such a pity that the exterior is so uninviting.

53

E.C.N. Building 1968

It was very clever of Dav to combine two subjects here into one picture. The apparent subject is the frame of the Eastern Counties Newspaper Building at Prospect Place but the real subject I suspect was the old Poultry Market – once a flourishing part of the Cattle Market scene before everything moved out to the 'agricultural Brasilia' at Harford.

The Poultry Market – a thing that I, for no accountable reason, hold in great affection – is now a garage while the E.C.N. Building has grown to become one of the wonders of Norwich. Floodlit at night, it looks like a Los Angeles cinema and is without question the most glamorous building in the City.

It is interesting that the scene depicted here illustrates both decline and growth. The Poultry Market, from where the picture is painted, reflects the decline of the importance of agriculture in the life of Norwich but the construction of the E.C.N. Building vividly demonstrates the growth of the City's importance as a centre of communication and of course the amazing recent growth of our local newspaper that a few years ago had a small office in London Street, then moved round the corner to Redwell Street before coming here.

Mousehold House c 1950

I am not sure when Dav painted this – from the style it must be very late 1940s or early 1950s – and what is even more irritating I don't know when the original house was built. I would place the date of its first construction at about 1760 and it was certainly restored in 1812. General Sir Robert Harvey – a hero of the Peninsular War – bought it shortly after Waterloo and had it extensively remodelled in 1821. He died in 1863 leaving £350,000 to his son who was a senior partner in Harvey and Hudsons Bank – the Crown Bank. He managed to lose his fortune and that of the Bank by backing France to win the Franco-Prussian War. When he realized his mistake, he shot himself on his estate at Crown Point.

continued on page 58

Mousehold House *continued from page 55*

In the 1870s the house was occupied by William Hackblock, a Director of Morgans Brewery. It was he who in 1881 had the first telephone in Norwich. A wire was suspended a distance of a mile and a half between Mousehold House and the Brewery in King Street. He was succeeded as tenant by another brewer, Mr Josiah Poyser a Northerner and a Director of Allsops and Sons of Burton-on-Trent.

In 1907 the house came into the possession of the Harbord family who occupied it until the 1960s. During that time various parts of the extensive estate were sold until eventually in 1930 Norwich Corporation bought the remainder – including the house.

In the 1960s it would undoubtedly have been demolished but for the unconventional efforts of Geoffrey Goreham who moved in as caretaker and fought for its preservation. In the end the house was saved and curiously many of those who were hell-bent on destroying it suddenly became its champions.

H.M.S.O. 1967

It was in early 1965 that we first heard officially that Her Majesty's Stationery Office was to move to Norwich and that its offices would be built on a site near to Stump Cross in Magdalen Street. The Development was to be one of the biggest in the City's history and would involve a shopping complex and the dreaded Magdalen Street Flyover that had been rearing its ugly head off and on for decades.

Work began in 1967 and Dav rushed over to the site to record the progress of construction. This painting, executed in black and grey, is in my opinion one of his best.

The New Odeon, Anglia Square   1971

I wonder how many people now remember all the bitterness that was aroused by the Council's plan for the Magdalen Street Flyover. Perhaps the controversy concerning the absurd and now withdrawn Timberhill Redevelopment Scheme has helped to make Anglia Square and its environs more acceptable. Whatever the reasons, nobody seems to have much to say about this new area of the City – except to express a grudging admiration of the way in which the Flyover has achieved its aim of easing traffic congestion.

But in fact I suspect that people are rather relieved that Anglia Square turned out to be not nearly so bad as we had been led to expect. It certainly has a sort of 'Space Age' attractiveness that appealed to Davenport and which I find irresistible.

The New Odeon stands above the Square and can be reached from the Flyover by a road that leads back to ground-level in Edwards Street. The whole Development is a place of supermarkets, launderettes, night-clubs, and Wimpy bars with a massive office block towering above on one side and a multi-storey car park on the other; it is as if the Developers had made a selection from a catalogue of the American Dream – but there's nothing wrong in that.

Standing in this twenty-first-century Peyton Place, especially on a sunny day, it is so easy to forget little old Botolph Street, Roberts' strange old printing-works, and the Toytown bank that stood at Stump Cross. I wonder if, given the chance, the people of Norwich would exchange Anglia Square for what stood there before. I rather doubt it.

60

King Street Brewery 1970

When a Norwich Lord Mayor of the 1930s was talking about the City Hall, which was then being built, he compared it with that of Stockholm. 'The vista from our City Hall tower however will be something completely different. It will be a vista of Breweries.' It was said with pride, for brewing has always been an industry here and still is today.

When the Lord Mayor spoke about the view from the City Hall tower, Norwich had four breweries which gradually amalgamated with one another. Then, at the beginning of the 1960s Watneys bought up Morgans, but they were not interested in owning pubs here and sold all the tied houses to Bullards and Steward and Pattersons. It was only the sudden large sales of Watneys beers – which were being sold by the local breweries at a much higher price than their own – that prompted Watneys to reconsider.

Watneys fortunately didn't close the brewery here but built a new one in King Street on the site of Morgans premises where a brewery had existed since before the Reformation.

This painting by Dav shows the Morgans building of 1947 with the bridge that Watneys put up in the late 1960s. It is not a beautiful building but it does look like a brewery and it fits in well with the down-to-earth industrial scenery of King Street. Further down the road is Reads flour-mill built in the early part of the last century as a yarn factory and on the opposite bank of the river is Boulton and Pauls.

And there among the industry is the architectural heritage of Norwich. The Old Music House believed to be the oldest existing dwelling-house in England, and the former town-house of the Howards – before they became Dukes of Norfolk. And the Old Barge – no longer a pub but maintained by the brewery and used by them for training personnel and for special occasions. This is the pleasing thing about Norwich – the way in which factories stand side by side with medieval houses and how well they seem to get on together.

Houses Being Demolished in Prospect Place   Mid 1960s

On the hillside between King Street and Ber Street, the Victorians built an overcrowded warren of cottages which by the middle of the present century had become totally unfit for human habitation. Here and there could be found a large house, built earlier than its neighbouring tenements, and there was a certain amount of Dickensian character lurking about the place, but in the early 1960s the Council embarked on its last major slum-clearance scheme and the whole area was swept away.

Dav's painting shows the houses near the Cattle Market – the site is now occupied by the offices of Eastern Counties Newspapers.

Balconies of No. 35 Surrey Street   1955

Nearly everybody should be able to recognize this piece of Victorian wrought-iron work. It forms the back of the house on the corner of Surrey Street and All Saints Green. You may deplore it but you can't help noticing it. Personally I rather like these balconies. They add a touch of human eccentricity and character to the Georgian symmetry of the house that Thomas Ivory built in 1761.

Railings by Thorpe Station   c 1970

This web of rails and posts which runs up a passageway beside Thorpe Station is typical of the kind of thing which caught Davenport's pictorial attention. Where most of us would pass unheeding, he saw pattern and potential pictures. This subject, moreover, was a real challenge to his power as a draughtsman and, for all its humdrum nature, by no means easy to draw.

He knew all the alleys and short-cuts on his routes round Norwich, some of them quite unofficial ones. As an avowed and veteran pedestrian or cyclist their discovery was not only a boon but a hobby, and he would often disclose them with pride and zest to his friends, recommending them for the time they saved or for the unexpected view they afforded.

This type of guard-rail was once a common sight in the city. A maze of them covered the old Cattle Market and some are still to be seen at the bottom of Bracondale where they provided pedestrian refuge from the herds of cattle which used to be driven through the streets from the railway yards at Trowse.

Gasworks in St Martin's Plain   early 1960s

This is one of the many paintings Dav did of the Gasworks in St Martin's Plain. The first Norwich Gasworks was built in St Stephen's Back Street (Malthouse Road) in 1820 but within ten years it had been moved to a site in Thorpe opposite Bishops Bridge.

The building seen here was erected in St Martin's Plain in 1851 and stood on the site of the house of Sir Thomas Erpingham. Many protests were raised over the years about the siting of a gasworks here but, after all, it had to be built somewhere and I believe that it is better to mix industry in with antiquity than to totally separate them. In fact this is what most people consider to be the charm of the city – the medieval church next to the shoe factory, the office block behind the Georgian house.

Anyway, the Gasworks is gone now and we will soon be able to see what improvement the Council is going to replace it with – so far the site has been used as a car park.

Britannia Barracks and Mousehold early 1950s

Mousehold is to Norwich what Hampstead Heath is to London, and much more besides. In 1549 it was the scene of one of the most fascinating rebellions in England's history when Robert Kett raised a peasant army of 20,000 and looked favourably placed to seize the Kingdom.

He called his army 'The King's Great Camp' and issued proclamations in the name of the young Edward VI, claiming all the time to be the King's most loyal subject. He held Norwich and defeated several Government attempts to dislodge him but after nine weeks the end came on 25 August, when he lost a battle with German and Italian mercenaries under the Earl of Warwick. But it is doubtful whether he could have been defeated if he had chosen to remain on Mousehold and had not moved his forces to the Wensum Valley below – the Vale of Dussindale – as an ancient prophecy had advised him. An even more interesting question is what would have happened if he had decided to move on London after his early victories.

In Kett's day the Heath stretched for several miles in all directions but during the last 150 years it has gradually shrunk. The picture shows Britannia Barracks built in 1886/87 and, on the left, the Ranger's House where Dav used to stop for a cup of tea on his Saturday morning walk. Beyond these buildings is the open Heath that he loved.

The Rosary Tavern c 1970

Until the building of the first Foundry Bridge in the 1840s Thorpe was cut off from Norwich by the Wensum. The only means of entry to the City was by Bishops Bridge. Riverside Road was, until 1900, just a towpath lined with trees and bushes and the main, indeed the only, built-up road between the City and Thorpe was Chalk Hill – now known as Rosary Road.

68

This had begun to be developed after the building of the Gasworks near Bishops Bridge in 1830. At the Thorpe end of the road was the Regency Rosary Cemetery – the first in Norwich – which gave the road its name. The older name of Chalk Hill (still perpetuated in the steep Chalk Hill Road) was derived from the Norman pits and caves from which some 20,000 yards of chalk had been cut for use as lime in the building of the Cathedral.

Later one of these pits was again to be used in the interests of 'Christianity'. It was shown on medieval and Tudor maps as 'Lollards Pit – the place where men are customarally burnt'. George Borrow wrote of it 'Many a saint of God has breathed his last beneath that white precipice, midst flame and pitch; many a grisly procession has advanced across the old bridge towards the Lollards Hole.'

A happier use was put to some of the land adjoining Rosary Road in 1908 when The Nest was opened as the ground of Norwich City Football Club. The Canaries stayed at The Nest until moving to Carrow Road in 1935.

The Rosary Tavern is typical of many of the quaint Victorian buildings that are dotted about here and the near-by area of St Leonards Road. Dav chose to paint this one but there are dozens of others that must have interested him as much as they do me and are all worth finding.

Timber-yards at Riverside Early 1950s

The River is a recurring theme in this or any other book about Norwich. Without it there would be no City. The Saxon pirates who founded the first settlement called it the 'Wendsome' because it wended its way through the hills of Norwich and the valleys of Norfolk. They stopped here because they couldn't navigate their boats beyond the area of Cowgate.

This timber-yard, backing on to King Street, stood on the site of the earliest part of Norwich – Conesford, the 'King's Ford'.

Over the centuries, the Wensum has provided the City's contact with the outside world and been its source of trade. The stones that built the Cathedral and Castle were carried along this waterway and the river provided the defences along the eastern and northern part of the City.

Today the Wensum is still a commercial highway but it is also a source of pleasure to visitors and citizens alike and, with the Council's scheme of riverside walks, scenes like the one above will become more and more rare.

St Helen's Church (The Great Hospital) Bishopsgate 1972

Norwich has several attractive approaches. One, and perhaps the best known, is from Cringleford Bridge, through the village of Eaton and along the great avenue of Newmarket Road. But that leads only to the Inner Ring Road and St Stephens Street. A better approach is from the east, from the heights of Thorpe or better still Mousehold and down into the valley below.

Crossing Bishops Bridge, one enters Bishopsgate and the whole of Norwich seems to be just round the corner. In front of you is the best view of the Cathedral and the Castle on the left of the skyline, around you is Norwich's past. Cow Tower is in the Great Meadow on the right and further down the road is the Great Hospital founded in 1249 and re-established by Henry VIII.

70

Most of the Church of St Helen forms part of the Hospital – which is really a collection of almshouses – and only the central part of the nave is used for religious services. Interestingly, the pulpit was put in the place of the altar during the Commonwealth and has not been moved since. Outside the church door is a sixteenth-century eulogy of the Tudors which reads:

King Henry the Eighth, of Noble Fame
Bequeath'd this City, this Commodious Place,
With Lands and Rents, he did Endow the same,
To help decreped Age in Woful Case.
Edward the Sixth that Prince of Royal Stem,
Perform'd his Fathers generous Bequest,
Good Queen Elizabeth imiatating them,
Ample Endowments added to the Rest.
Their pious Deeds we gratefully record,
While Heaven them crowns with glorious Reward.

Bishops
Bridge
1946

Bishops Bridge   1946

Bishops Bridge is the only surviving medieval bridge in the City. Dav painted it in 1946 soon after he arrived in Norwich. He little realized that one day he would live a stone's throw away.

It is a part of Norwich which everybody knows, admires, and likes. It was built not by the Bishop of Norwich as many people think, but by that great citizen Richard Spynk who, between 1337 and 1344 completed the walls, gates, and defences of the City at his own expense. For this magnificent act of loyalty he and his descendants were 'quitted of all tax and tollage, etc. for all time'.

Until then the river-crossing at this point had consisted of timbers laid on stone piers. The bulging arches at the west end of the bridge were built by Spynk to support the Gatehouse that stood above. But although the Bishop didn't build the bridge he still had the control over it until 1393 when the City took over its jurisdiction and let the chamber in the Gatehouse for five shillings a year.

During Kett's Rebellion, the bridge changed hands several times as Civic, Rebel, and Government forces gained control. Nicholas Sotherton's contemporary account of the Rebellion says that when Kett was trying to capture the City he sent 'vagabond boys, naked and unarmed', across the river here. They

74

ran among the enemy archers and seized arrows to return to their own side. They even plucked arrows from their bodies and legs and handed them, still dripping with blood, to the rebel archers who fired them at the enemy.

These boys' utter contempt for danger 'so dismayed the archers (within the City) that it took the heart from them'.

The Gatehouse survived until 1790 when the Corporation asked two gentlemen named Dove and Wilkins (the latter did a great deal of work on the Castle) to examine it. They did so and reported that the arches of the bridge were cracking under the strain of the tower's weight. The Gatehouse was consequently demolished in the following year at a cost of £170.

Bishops Bridge and the Red Lion 1970

The opposite painting was executed over twenty years after the first one and shows how Dav's style had changed. By this time of course, he lived at 54 Bishopsgate and the Red Lion, on the left of the picture, was his 'local'.

The Hermitage 1972 (overleaf)

This painting shows Dav's house from the garden. The house, known as The Hermitage, is at 54 Bishopsgate and is over 500 years old. It was once the vicarage of the Church of St Mary in the Marsh – the parish church of The Close – which disappeared four centuries ago.

The Sunflower

In recent years, Dav had taken to painting sunflowers. They were always sunflowers and something – *Sunflower and Cathedral, Sunflower and Power Station* - this one is called *Sunflower and House*. The house in question was 54 Bishopsgate, perhaps better known as 'The Hermitage', which was its proper name. It was Davenport's home although nobody could be less like a hermit than he was.

There are many stories of Dav, all fantastic, nearly all true, which go some way towards explaining why this man was so famous and so popular with so many people. Of course, he must have had his faults but it's hard to think what they were. He wasn't a saint – 'old devil' is how he was more often described but there was something about Dav that brought an air of happiness wherever he went. I recall one evening when he appeared in the 'Queen Vic' wearing a top hat and a cauliflower in his buttonhole. 'Cauliflower-power, man!' he shouted. It wasn't sophisticated humour but it was a mixture of satire and slapstick that suited him well. As it happened, he appeared in the same pub a few days later wearing an elastic band round his bald head. Characteristically he never explained it and affected not to hear questions about it. He was still wearing it when he left the pub.

His pub singing was another aspect of Dav – and the one that I knew first. It was in the Queen Victoria in Magdalen Street (a pub now demolished) that I first saw him perform. His biggest hit and signature-tune was 'I've got no pants on!' sung to the tune 'I'm the Sheik of Araby' but he also rendered 'My old man's a dustman' with special choruses of his own creation. Yet he could shout his way through 'The White Cliffs of Dover' and, despite the bizarre lyrics he invented, produce the same sort of nostalgic effect as if Vera Lynn had stood in the public bar and sung it straight. 'Jingle Bells' was another favourite of his, once he had tampered with the words.

Later I came to see the other Dav – or rather the other Davs for there were many facets to his character. He was a serious figure, not just in art but in the social life of Norwich – even in the history of Norwich. He seriously cared about the causes he believed in but he always shunned serious*ness* – that is why he became the man he was. He entertained us and injected a cheerfulness into any group he came in contact with. He was a person who wasn't afraid of making a fool of himself and consequently he never *did*, despite the bizarre postures he affected. If evidence were needed of how seriously he is now considered it is sufficient to note that a retrospective exhibition of his work is being held as part of the Triennial Festival and that this book was written as a memento of him.

Davenport was not a native of Norwich. Fate cast him here and like the sunflower he took root and enlivened our City.

Printed in Great Britain by Galliard (Printers) Ltd Great Yarmouth